the seeds of self-destruction or SUCCESS

the seeds of self-destruction or **SUCCESS**

ingredients | absolutes | possibilites

Charles L Blanchard

Copyright © 2023 Charles L Blanchard.

All rights reserved. No part of this book may be used or reproduced by any means, graphic, electronic, or mechanical, including photocopying, recording, taping or by any information storage retrieval system without the written permission of the author except in the case of brief quotations embodied in critical articles and reviews.

This book is a work of non-fiction. Unless otherwise noted, the author and the publisher make no explicit guarantees as to the accuracy of the information contained in this book and in some cases, names of people and places have been altered to protect their privacy.

Archway Publishing books may be ordered through booksellers or by contacting:

Archway Publishing
1663 Liberty Drive
Bloomington, IN 47403
www.archwaypublishing.com
844-669-3957

Because of the dynamic nature of the Internet, any web addresses or links contained in this book may have changed since publication and may no longer be valid. The views expressed in this work are solely those of the author and do not necessarily reflect the views of the publisher, and the publisher hereby disclaims any responsibility for them.

Any people depicted in stock imagery provided by Getty Images are models, and such images are being used for illustrative purposes only. Certain stock imagery © Getty Images.

Scripture texts in this work are taken from the New American Bible, revised edition © 2010, 1991, 1986, 1970 Confraternity of Christian Doctrine, Washington, D.C. and are used by permission of the copyright owner. All Rights Reserved. No part of the New American Bible may be reproduced in any form without permission in writing from the copyright owner.

ISBN: 978-1-6657-3746-3 (sc)
ISBN: 978-1-6657-3745-6 (hc)
ISBN: 978-1-6657-3747-0 (e)

Library of Congress Control Number: 2023901101

Print information available on the last page.

Archway Publishing rev. date: 01/21/2023

May *The Seeds of Self-Destruction or Success* be dedicated to Harry R. Posner Jr., my beautiful one, and our girls, Heidi Marie, Rosie Jean, Cecilia Yvette Carmel, and Sophia Catherine Laboure, for helping me to appreciate, see, and know what always was here: love.

Contents

Foreword	ix
PART I: THE INGREDIENTS OF LIFE	**1**
Preface	3
Chapter 1: The Roots of Mistrust	5
Chapter 2: Shame and Doubt Reign Supreme	7
Chapter 3: The Guilt Begins	9
Chapter 4: The Vail of Inferiority Begins to Lift	17
PART II: FEEDING THE WHOLE—MIND, BODY, AND SOUL (The World of Absolutes)	**23**
Preface	25
Chapter 5: Leaving Home	27
Chapter 6: The Winds of Change	31
Chapter 7: Blowing Open the Doors	40
Chapter 8: Becoming Uncloseted . . . Again	45
Chapter 9: Duality	47
Chapter 10: The Year of Living Dangerously	49
Chapter 11: "To Where Are You Going?"	50
Chapter 12: Not Exactly a Return to Innocence	53
Chapter 13: The Fall from Grace	59
Chapter 14: Focus, Fortitude, and Forbearance	62

PART III: LIVING LIFE ANEW
(The World of Possibilities)   **71**

Chapter 15: Rising Above Life's Challenges	73
Chapter 16: Embracing "What Good Looks Like"	75
Chapter 17: "Where There Are No Resources, Create Them"	89
Chapter 18: Who Are Your ANGELs?	95
Acknowledgments	99
Bibliography	103
About the Author	105

Foreword

by Lloyd Sam Cunningham

When we wake up in the morning, we never quite know who we are going to meet on our day's journey or if our shared experience is going to become an impressed memory in our minds, giving each person importance for the full journey of our lives. For me, I probably won't understand the significance of that encounter until I take it in, with reflection, as I imbibe with coffee and God. Somehow, that journey and reflection has brought me into repeated encounters with Charles L. Blanchard. Some of these are with coffee, some of them are with pizza, some of them are just in prayer, and now, it is through the memoirs of his life. When Charles met me, I was a Roman Catholic priest working in vocation and Hispanic ministry. He was a college seminarian whom I met through mutual friends. We became friends. We would meet every so often, usually socially, but later, at church, when he and Harry came to town. At that time, I was one of the liturgical coordinators for AGLO Chicago (i.e., the Archdiocesan Gay and Lesbian Outreach for the Archdiocese of Chicago) on weekends while I completed doctoral studies in clinical psychology at what is today, Adler University.

Charles and Harry would bring me up to speed about their lives as we had dinner after Eucharist. I found their journey grace-filled as they endeavored to understand how God was and is working in their lives. A little less than a year ago, Charles informed me that at the urging of his spiritual companion, he was writing a self-help book and personal memoir about his journey that was leading him to overcome the obstacles of childhood abuse, a traumatic dog attack, homophobia, and now chronic illness through shared faith and love with family, friends, parishioners, and his husband, Harry. He honored me with the question, would I read it and write the foreword? I was stunned and blessed at the same time.

As a psychologist who often teaches developmental psychology, I was immediately taken by his reference at the very beginning to the developmental stages of Erik Erikson. Charles, in the first chapters of his book, uses Erikson's stages to show us how the actual ingredients of our lives—because of childhood abuse and other traumatic experiences—may foster mistrust instead of trust, shame and guilt instead of autonomy, guilt instead of initiative, inferiority instead of industry, and role confusion instead of identity. Charles, through the experiences of having a mom, stepfather, a newfound faith, new friends, and purpose, found new seeds in his life that have grown generativity and intimacy for him. What you will read in this book is an expression of Charles's generativity, which at the same time reveals the sacramental intimacy of Charles and Harry, mirroring God's love to each other.

In teaching psychology, it is always easy to find the stories of how personal experiences lead some to failure. However, *The Seeds of Self-Destruction or Success* presents, in a very personal way, how Charles is able overcome the binary of nature and nurture through conscious decisions encouraged by positive people on his journey. The relationships he has found, especially with his husband, have led, at this juncture of his life, to find trust and hope rather than mistrust and despair.

Charles, as an author, in his present priestly ministry, writes for us, who are constantly hearing stories of self-destruction, a way to find trust, love, and hope instead of despair. I will recommend this book to both my theology and psychology students and give them an example of how mentors, friends, and lovers can lead us and others to overcome the obstacles of abuse, and how truly loving relationships, even same-sex relationships, can reflect God's love. The book and friendship of the author are blessing to me.

Fellow Journeyer,
Lloyd Sam Cunningham, SVD, MDiv, PsyD, HSP

Part I

THE INGREDIENTS OF LIFE

Preface

I woke up in the closet.

It wasn't a confused or disoriented awakening, stirring to find a reality I didn't recognize; I chose to sleep there. Despite the limited ability to escape if needed, burrowing deep within the confines of those four walls felt somehow safe. Or as safe as I could feel in our house.

For the first seven years of my life, my house was not a home. At least, not in the conventional sense. Of course, what is conventional? We never truly know what happens behind the closed doors of others'. And we certainly can't claim to understand the intricacies of each person's story behind those doors. What I can say for certain is that it's very complicated. And my house was no different.

So, I hid in the closet. It was the only place I could shelter myself from the wrath of my father. And as the beatings increased, so too, did the time I spent there. Of course, being in the closet would become a poignantly familiar theme in my life—an irony that is not lost on me. And the fact that I was a "special" boy (a euphemism, to be sure) seemed only to fuel my father's rage all the more.

My house would eventually become a home, in as much as I would feel safe there. But that would require the extraction of my father and many days and nights of fleeing, fear, and terror before that.

Out of the dark reaches of that closet, who could have imagined a life full of successes and a sense of feeling settled? It seemed so far away then. So impossible.

I didn't know to whom I could go to disclose the physical beatings and abuse my father administered. I couldn't imagine any adult would ever believe a three-year-old saying that he and his mother were being attacked, physically injured, and beaten by the man who was supposed to be his father and her husband. You see, at that time, I needed to avoid the shame and the ever-present and unpredictable lurch of physical pain. I had to keep it all a secret.

To make some sense of this dangerous person in my house, I turned to the Warner Brothers and their *Looney Tunes*. More specifically, the Tasmanian devil. "Taz" was billed as an unpredictable life force that destroyed anything and everything within its path. From my perspective, the Tasmanian devil was very much the less-than-kind biological father I knew.

Thus, I began to refer to him—at least behind his back—as Taz. It was a well-deserved title. And it helped me make sense of the madness in my house.

chapter one

The Roots of Mistrust

∎

Erikson's First Stage of Psychosocial Development Trust versus Mistrust

From birth to twelve months of age, infants must learn that adults can be trusted. This occurs when adults meet a child's basic needs for survival. Infants are dependent upon their caregivers, so caregivers who are responsive and sensitive to their infant's needs help their baby to develop a sense of trust; their baby will see the world as a safe, predictable place. Unresponsive caregivers who do not meet their baby's needs can engender feelings of anxiety, fear, and mistrust; their baby may see the world as unpredictable. If infants are treated cruelly or their needs are not met appropriately, they will likely grow up with a sense of mistrust for people in the world.[1]

It's hard to say when the beatings began. It's also difficult to say what series of events were responsible for creating the man who was my father. But there are likely parallels to my own experience as a son. I know that he had two brothers and a sister. And I also know that they lost their mother at an early age. Their father raised them alone and on a tight budget. And this was at a time when it was exceedingly rare for a father to step into a maternal or nurturing role—a role he likely resented. His childhood was probably difficult, and in turn, he made mine exceedingly difficult. He was most likely a product of his environment, and my mother and I paid the price for his woundedness.

I feel it's important to remember that each of us entering a situation comes through a different door and with our own unique life experiences. I've had to do this with my father. Based on this scant understanding of his childhood, it's safe to assume that it left deep wounds that he could not overcome. Rather than processing life's challenges, he stayed in a state of rage, lashing out at those he was supposed to love. This does not in any way justify my father's beatings, mind you. But it does help me to remember that he was most likely also a victim at one time.

Whatever the case, when I was born on that cold January 16, in 1965, a lot of my father's story was already written. And just as is the case with all children and their parents, it certainly would impact my own story.

chapter two

Shame and Doubt Reign Supreme

∎

Erikson's Second Stage of Psychosocial Development: Autonomy versus Shame/Doubt

As toddlers (ages one to three years) begin to explore their world, they learn that they can control their actions and act on their environment to get results. They begin to show clear preferences for certain elements of the environment, such as food, toys, and clothing. A toddler's main task is to resolve the issue of autonomy vs. shame and doubt by working to establish independence. This is the "me do it" stage. For example, we might observe a budding sense of autonomy in a two-year-old child who wants to choose her clothes and dress herself. Although her outfits might not be appropriate for the situation, her input in such basic decisions has an effect on her sense of independence. If denied the opportunity to act on her environment, she may begin to doubt her abilities, which could lead to low self-esteem and feelings of shame.[2]

When I came along, my older sister was used to receiving most of the attention. She was daddy's girl, and I wasn't exactly the son he wanted. This was, of course, to be expected. The roots of sibling rivalry are established early. What was less expected, however, was the rivalry my father immediately experienced with me. I was a breech birth and, by all accounts, a sickly child. While some fathers would naturally default to instinctive nurturing, my father saw my struggles as a weakness and a threat. He seemed to resent that I would require more attention from my mother, Catherine Jean.

To make matters worse, I was born with a dislocated hip. Of course, this wouldn't come to light until I learned to walk with a rather noticeable limp. Unfortunately, by that time, my hip had fused. So at the age of two, they had to break it. This left me in a body cast from the waist down, which kept my lower body in captivity for a year. There was a bar that extended between my feet to set my hips properly. Still, it's pretty tough to keep a two-year-old still. To get around, I quickly adopted an effective "GI Joe crawl"—pulling myself along on alternating elbows as I dragged that heavy cast around. The human body's ability to adapt is truly amazing.

I have no memory of my time in the cast. This is probably fortunate, because I suspect that it was painful at times. And what made it all the more painful was my father's continued resentment of me. He seemed to think, at the ripe age of two, that I had willed this condition upon myself purely to spite him and to steal my mother's attention. I can only imagine what impact this had on my older sister. Although she was only three and a half, she probably felt some resentment as well—given that my mother had to spend so much time taking care of me.

Perhaps this is where my father first began to find a connection with my sister and to fashion an ally out of her. He would eventually form a bond with my younger sister as well, utilizing all the manipulations of a classic abuser to ensure that he was seen in a good light by those who mattered to him.

chapter three

The Guilt Begins

■

Erikson's Third Stage of Psychosocial Development: Initiative versus Guilt

Once children reach the preschool stage (ages three to six years), they are capable of initiating activities and asserting control over their world through social interactions and play. According to Erikson, preschool children must resolve the task of initiative vs. guilt. By learning to plan and achieve goals while interacting with others, preschool children can master this task. Initiative, a sense of ambition and responsibility, occurs when parents allow a child to explore within limits and then support the child's choice. These children will develop self-confidence and feel a sense of purpose. Those who are unsuccessful at this stage—with their initiative misfiring or stifled by over-controlling parents—may develop feelings of guilt.[3]

And, of course, my sisters saw my father in a good light. Why wouldn't they? He cared for and was always kind to them. They slept upstairs and were insulated from the sounds of abuse that echoed through the main floor of our house, where I slept. In other words, he was a father to them, or at least what they understood a father to be. To begrudge them this would have served no one. But that still didn't make it easy.

My father never once beat my sisters. Of the three children, he reserved those beatings solely for me. But he also beat my mother, and I think she took many beatings that were intended for me. She attempted to protect me as best she could, although, in reality, any time my father beat my mother, it was also an assault on me. I am sure she would say the same thing. It could not have been easy for her to witness her son being abused, but she was trapped. Times are different today than they were during my childhood.

As the beatings became more frequent, I spent more time in the closet. There were three particularly violent incidents that stick in my mind to this day. Two of them happened to my mother, and one of them to me.

The first incident was when my mother attempted to escape to the bathroom and was subsequently bludgeoned in the bathtub after my father broke down the door. This experience is etched in my mind and has haunted me throughout my formative years. To this day, the sight of my bloodied mother begging for mercy eats at me and causes resentment against my father.

And then there was the night he picked me up by the back of my shirt like a suitcase and threw me against the wall. I not only remember his rage but I also remember feeling his hatred. He threw me like one would discard trash. This incident was different than the other times he beat me. It was more than the usual abuse; as he threw me, it was clear that he wished I was not part of his life. To him, I was not his son; I was a disappointment, or perhaps

the seeds of self-destruction or SUCCESS

a symbol of his inadequacy as a man and as a father. Perhaps he saw something in me that he disliked in himself.

The last incident marked the end of the abuse. It was the last straw that motivated my mother to stop the insanity. My parents were fighting in the hallway near my bedroom, and my father was beating my mom. While attempting to intervene, my maternal grandmother became the target instead. My mother overcame her fear and mustered the strength to strike him in the head with an iron skillet, nearly killing him. As he lay motionless on the floor all night, she finally did it. She broke free and filed for divorce. The abuse ended, but the memories still haunted us.

When we speak of abuse, it often involves a cyclical pattern, and it was no different in my home. Nearly every time my father beat my mother and me, we would flee to a place of safety, but we would inevitably return, and the cycle would play itself out repeatedly.

In fact, there were an increasing number of nights that my mother would whisk us all away to stay with her mother or her sister to protect us. She would never seek refuge at the home of her father, though. This is likely because, as is the norm for those who are abused, she still felt the need to protect my father, or perhaps she felt a level of shame for finding herself in such a situation.

My grandfather was the captain of detectives in the local police department, and had he known, he would have put an end to the abuse. He was a good man, but the fact that his daughter and grandson were being abused would have been too much for him to manage. His manner of stopping the abuse may have crossed the line, or at least that was a fear my mother shared with me later in life. One thing is certain: had he known what was happing in our house, it would have ended one way or another.

As for those of us living under that roof, we'd come to normalize this occasional "fleeing" in the night to the homes of other relatives. My sisters had all but blocked out the attacks at home, as denial was their way of coping. Going to my grandma's or aunt's became like a minivacation. We'd stay for a bit, maybe a day or two. It was nice there. There was plenty of cooking, and my sisters and I would swim a lot. We'd ride bikes and go golfing with my step-grandfather—which essentially meant he'd go golfing and we'd catch the balls. We'd run around the basement and, well, be children. I felt free and unburdened. Unafraid. And except for worrying about wetting the bed there, those were some of the happiest times I remember.

Eventually, we'd have to go back home, though. I dreaded the return every minute. And soon, the cycle would start again. This was just how we did things. At the age of five, six, and seven, I simply didn't question it. And neither did my sisters. Normalizing these events was our natural best defense.

Another thing I normalized was the relative absence of my paternal grandfather. He wasn't dead; he was simply not a participant in my life. I have little to no memory of him. So be it. Some say that blood makes you related, but loyalty makes you family. I've come to learn that as adults, we have the ability to choose those we consider family, but children don't have that choice.

Fortunately, as a result of my mother's parents divorcing and subsequently remarrying, I still had two sets of grandparents. They were fully present in my life. My grandma and grandpa Clemens would throw us birthday parties when we were young. They symbolized stability, love, and affection, and would later be actively involved in supporting my seminary goals. My relationship with my grandma and grandpa Smith was different, but still loving. They were leaders and revered in their community. I idolized Grandpa Smith. He represented stability, strength, and courage—the polar opposite of my father. I looked up to my grandparents and am eternally grateful for their presence in my life.

I also had connections with other family members, like my cousin Bill. It was with Bill that I had one of my earliest childhood memories, and it's not a particularly cheerful one. I was only five years old. We had gone to visit his grandmother. The details are sketchy, as they often are in such an old memory, but I remember being in the backseat of a car and told to stay there because Bill's grandma had a mean dog. So, there I sat. I can't say how long I was sitting there, but eventually his grandma came out to the car and assured me that the dog would do me no harm.

I was no stranger to pain at that point in my life, and I'd certainly been "betrayed" by adults. But for whatever reason, I chose to trust her. So off I went with her and into the house. The last thing I remember is the dog lunging at me—as if in slow motion—through a group of adults. After that, everything went black.

The dog had taken my face in its jaws and would not let go. It took a fierce beating with a bat to get him to release his grip on my head. Had the dog not eventually died from that brutal beating, he would have been euthanized. But they still had to send his head to Lansing to ensure that he didn't have rabies. Fortunately, he didn't. I later learned that dog was also a victim of merciless teasing from neighborhood children. We shared a difficult story, and both of us paid a heavy price.

It would take three reconstructive surgeries to get my face back. My mother, sisters, grandparents, aunts, and uncle came to be with me—which was of great comfort—but my father never came, nor did my paternal grandfather. The one thing that I distinctly remember from that experience was the time I was alone in the hospital and the overwhelming sense of fear and loneliness I experienced.

In retrospect, it probably wasn't a great deal of time that I was alone. But an hour to a five-year-old is infinitely longer than it is to an adult. And I believe that it was in those spans of time that I was alone, that I began to finally grasp that I had a father who didn't love me. And he never would. From that day forward, I stopped trying to earn his love and emotionally distanced myself from him. In a sense, I divorced him before my mother did.

I still have a scar near my right eye from that dog bite. But I don't see it as a wound or a flaw. I see it more as a symbol of victory. It represents another obstacle I overcame, because there's simply no value in seeing myself as the perpetual victim. It's a dark place from which nothing can grow.

I've come to accept that I may never know exactly why my father and I didn't bond. As I said before, his story was already partly written by the time I came along. The many events that preceded my birth surely formed him. What I do know is that I wasn't what anyone would call an "average boy." Far from it, actually. And this likely came as a huge disappointment to him.

My mother and all my grandparents who spent time with me as a young child describe me in similar terms. I was sweet and quiet, tender and affectionate, smiling, docile, and even effeminate. In other words, I was far more sugar and spice than snips and snails. I was everything nice, versus puppy-dog tails. And my father was ashamed.

I was also fastidious and something of a neat freak. Clothes were neatly folded; my bed was always made.

Of course, I knew very early on I was gay—though this term wasn't in my vocabulary until much later. By the age of five, all I knew was that I was different. I liked playing dress-up in my mother's clothes. I was far less interested in playing doctor with the girls in my neighborhood than my other male friends were. I just wanted to make cakes in their Easy Bake Ovens and play with their dolls. I began to experiment with my friends, as many children do. I knew on some level that all of this was considered wrong, but it made perfect sense to me.

Still, it was all very confusing. For me, and for my father, I'm sure. But that confusion can never remotely justify the pain he caused me.

chapter four

The Vail of Inferiority Begins to Lift

■

Erikson's Third Stage of Psychosocial Development Initiative vs. Guilt

"During the elementary school stage (ages six to twelve), children face the task of industry vs. inferiority. Children begin to compare themselves with their peers to see how they measure up. They either develop a sense of pride and accomplishment in their schoolwork, sports, social activities, and family life, or they feel inferior and inadequate because they feel that they don't measure up. If children do not learn to get along with others or have negative experiences at home or with peers, an inferiority complex might develop into adolescence and adulthood."[4]

When I was seven, my mother finally left my father for good. There would be no more beatings and no more fleeing in the middle of the night. My house became a safe place. It became a home. It was during this time that I learned to cook and clean. I took to the garden with my mother, who finally had a chance to plant flowers. And despite her having to work three jobs because my father refused to send any money, she instituted a regular routine that helped me feel grounded for the first time in my life. She was always home at night for us to have dinner together, and my grandparents stayed with us during the times she had to be at work.

There was one huge drawback to my parents' divorce: in the year that followed, my father insisted on spending time with the kids. This meant that I'd have to be in his company without the safety of my mother. It was extremely upsetting to me. So, while my sisters rejoiced in their visits with him, I dreaded them. He would take us fishing—which he knew I disliked, particularly the barbaric act of hooking the worm. Meanwhile, my sisters—who loved fishing—made him proud. I, on the other hand, continued to be a disappointment.

Eventually, I was no longer required be part of these visits, though he continued to take my sisters fishing and out to restaurants. I chose to stay in the safety of my home, away from the man I had learned to fear and distrust. I suspect that my father was as satisfied with this arrangement as I was. As far as I was concerned, I didn't need a father. Not if my father was any indication of what a father was.

And just as I was becoming adjusted to my life without a father, Jack arrived. Jack was kind, stern, and steady. He loved my mother. He treated her well. And he treated *me* well. He would soon become the father I never had—even if he appeared ten years late. I say *appeared* because divine intervention works in mysterious ways. Just when you start thinking all hope is lost, it peers around the corner and steps back into your life. Jack's entry into my life would prove to be quite pivotal. And, honestly, the timing was probably right on. Because had I been younger, it may not have had the same impact.

Jack would be one of my greatest teachers at a time when I desperately needed one. He became the dad I needed and wanted in life. While my sisters called him *Jack*, I referred to him as *Dad*.

Jack was Roman Catholic. And despite my mother's lack of regard for religion, his was important to him—enough so that he arranged to have both his and my mother's divorces annulled so that their union would be recognized by the Catholic Church. Eventually, my mother also embraced the Catholic faith and became active in her parish.

With Jack, our home finally felt complete and my mother didn't need to worry so much about money anymore—although that didn't stop her from working. She actually enjoyed bookkeeping and waiting tables—especially when these jobs were no longer performed out of necessity. Jack brought a much-needed lightness into all our lives. Like many a father, he encouraged me to play sports. I liked soccer but didn't care at all for football. And although I liked basketball, I was not particularly good at it, although I did score two points once, but unfortunately, it was for the other team. I just saw an open basket and went for it. What can I say?

But here's the thing: Jack did not criticize me for the things others saw as shortcomings. He embraced me just as I was. He was a kind and patient teacher, creating learning experiences from any transgressions. He gently scolded me when he caught me hitting my younger sister—explaining that it was never OK to hurt others and that there were other ways to resolve conflict. Of course, that was good parenting. But I think that it was also very much intended to ensure I didn't repeat the pattern of abuse—as is so often the case with children who are abused. And because I revered him, I was able to hear his words and call him *Dad*.

This reverence was likely what sparked my interest in the Catholic Church too. Around the time of Jack's arrival, I began to attend Catholic services with my neighborhood friend and his family. I loved it. Of course, the fact that I was part of a family—a *real* family—was a strong draw. But it was more than that. I loved the music and the togetherness. I adored the mysterious quality of mass. And I relished the fact that I had something to look forward to each week.

What I didn't realize was how hungry I was for the structure, stability, and discipline that the church gave me. Something in me awakened, and after I finished my fifth-grade year in the public school system, I decided I would transfer to St. Mary's Catholic School for sixth grade. It would be the greatest decision I made in my young life.

I was finally in my element. Despite being academically deficient at my old school, life at my new school felt whole. It was a new beginning where people were kind, welcoming, and open. And I began to blossom under the care of the religious sisters and the parish priest. So, I decided right then and there that I wanted to be a priest. I was told I was going to have to wait until the eighth grade to go into seminary.

It was at St. Mary's School where I began to understand what it meant to achieve. In the sixth grade, I had my Catholic baptism. I also became the top candy salesperson by creating preorder forms, canvasing the neighborhood and local businesses, and thereby ensuring success. By the eighth grade, I was elected president of the student council and had curried some serious favor with the sisters, faculty, and classmates. But more importantly, it was there where I first recognized God's call to priesthood.

So, by the end of the eighth grade, I was thirteen years old and was getting ready to start seminary. It felt like the dark days were behind me and my life was finally on track. Of course, the repercussions of those days were yet to come, but at least I no longer sought refuge in my bedroom closet. And for that, I was grateful. It was progress. And all victories—no matter how big or small—should be celebrated.

It's funny, really. My memory of that childhood house is of how very big it was. But not too long ago, I had the chance to see the house, which is now abandoned. In my adult view, it was anything *but* big. And as I peered into the windows, I got a glimpse of that closet that felt so large and all-consuming in its ability to be my safe haven.

In reality, it was very small. But bigger things were definitely on the horizon.

Part I I

FEEDING THE WHOLE—
MIND, BODY, AND SOUL
(The World of Absolutes)

Preface

Although an environment dominated by peace, warmth, and light nurtures growth, there's something to be said for the chaos and darkness that dominated the first thirteen years of my life. In fact, I'm quite certain they are largely responsible for my becoming a priest. Because, you see, to escape such torture, I needed to run. And it was to the stability and security of the Roman Catholic Church that I ran.

I'd like to say that I never looked back, but I would have to. Eventually.

chapter five

Leaving Home

■

In 1979, at the age of fourteen, I saw my trajectory only as forward moving. Sitting in the back seat of the car—with my mother and Jack in the front—we were heading south along the highway to Perrysburg, Ohio. In a separate car on that same highway, my grandparents Clemens were accompanying us. I felt like my whole life was starting over. And indeed, it was. I was going to attend Divine Word High School Seminary, and I could hardly contain myself.

I'd been newly baptized just two years before in the sixth grade by Father Henry William Berkemeier. Father Berkemeier was my parish priest, but he'd also been in charge of the grade school—which meant I'd been under his tutelage from sixth to eighth grade. I couldn't have asked for a more inspirational figure. He was sturdy, prayerful, and respected in the community. He was also theologically conservative. To me, he represented purity. And he inspired me to want to be like him as a priest.

I thought of him that morning as I was preparing to enter the seminary to study for priesthood. And though the excitement was palpable, I was justifiably scared that I was leaving Jack, my mom, my sisters, and my grandparents. As with all huge decisions, I couldn't help but think that maybe I was making a huge mistake.

But then we pulled up to the school. Located along the Maumee River, Divine Word Seminary was like a beacon. The school consisted of four massive buildings constructed in solid brick and shimmering glass, sitting on 374 acres of scenic land. One building housed the priests. Another building held the dining room and chapel, with a basement where all the goods were delivered. Classrooms, offices, and the student dormitory comprised the third building. This also happened to be where the dean of students lived. And the fourth building was a gymnasium. All four buildings were connected by underground tunnels. The grounds surrounding these stately structures were stunning as well. Unbeknown to me, my love of gardening would flourish in my four years there. The gardener was a religious brother, Brother Longinus, originally from Germany, who would share his wisdom of plants with me.

Upon reaching the door of the seminary, we were greeted by a towering African American man who welcomed us warmly. My narrow view of black people at that point had been formed by the confines of my neighborhood, where racism thrived. It pains me now to admit it, but, up until that point, I had never experienced diversity, and my friendships and life experience were limited to primarily white working-class people. My worldview was about to be challenged in a positive way. Time, education, and formation effected positive change in my life.

Seminary would change my view on so many things. I quickly came to see that there was a world beyond my childhood neighborhood, and I don't just mean Perrysburg, Ohio. In the seminary, I had the opportunity to travel. Yes, I'd start to travel the expanses of my mind and my beliefs, but I was able to physically travel as well. Since religious priests and brothers live in community, it was important that seminary students make sojourns to visit parishes and local communities in different parts of Ohio and Michigan, as well as in states farther flung.

Our local trips were chaperoned by Father McGurk, while the longer journeys were with Father Bob Jones and Brother Donald Champagne. We'd also make frequent trips to the Mother House in Techny, Illinois. The Mother House is the official residence of the Society of the Divine Word.

As I was finding new confidence in seminary, I was also finding my voice too. Literally. I took piano and voice with Brother Don Champagne. He was not only one of my teachers, but also my mentor. He helped to train me in music theory and appreciation. He has an inviting laughter and a deep baritone voice that almost belies his kind and sensitive nature. And at eighty years of age, he is still playing the organ and singing with great vibrancy. I would be blessed to have Brother Champagne as my mentor all the way through college seminary. Brother Don was a positive influence on my life, and I am grateful to still call him my friend so many years later.

I finished Divine Word High School Seminary in 1983. And with the exceptions of one big food fight and a minor traffic infraction, I graduated mostly without incident. And then, at eighteen years old and on my own, I was just brimming with hope and big plans. College would begin that fall, and I was hungry to continue my studies.

But college would bring with it its own unique challenges.

chapter six

The Winds of Change

■

College was a time of promise, especially in those first two years.

In 1983, I headed west from Perrysburg, Ohio, to Epworth, Iowa, to attend Divine Word College Seminary. While Perrysburg was hardly a metropolis, it seemed cosmopolitan compared to Epworth. Epworth, Iowa, was about twenty miles from the Mississippi River. It was essentially a one-light town with a pizza parlor, sitting quietly on a plain with some modest hills and curves.

The college was located off Highway 20—a long expanse of road that served as my running track. Yes, I'd become an avid runner in college, something to which Brother Don had introduced me. It was quiet and meditative and gave me time to sort my thoughts. Nonrunners often jokingly ask runners, "From what are you running?" When faced with this question, I would always just laugh and brush if off. The reality is, I was running from something that I wasn't yet fully ready to tackle and I didn't want to admit it. I would soon come to refer to Highway 20 as "my highway of comfort (MHC)." It was where I went when I wanted to find that particular brand of comfort that comes from running away.

Yet, the rigorous demands of college and the routine of seminary life wouldn't afford me the opportunity to keep hiding. And this is apparent in the assignment I wrote for my English composition class in 1984. I've included the paper here for you to read. Even as a young college student, I knew I was searching. I knew I had painful memories that needed to be processed.

A Unique Transitional Experience with God

Spirit and *Enthusiasm*, that is, life, that often possesses my body has been on a coffee break the last couple of weeks.

Confusion and *Frustration*, that is, death, wanting to gain control and justify the body, have seemingly initiated once again the process of exploiting the natural characteristics of my personality.

Why?

How can I allow such abuse to dominate and control my life?

Basically, I don't know!

Contrary to this blatantly simplistic answer, one day, God made a powerful difference!

The day was Friday, March 9, 1984.

It seemed to be another regular conditioned day at Divine Word College Seminary as I awoke with the bitter, biting, and dry taste of yesterday's pains and hurts.

The alarm went off at 6:45 a.m. with a loud and annoying sound that said, "Time to get your rear end out of bed for another fun-filled day at divine word college seminary and remember morning prayers are in forty-five minutes!"

Now, who in the hell feels like singing and praising God at the "bloody" hour of the day? Precisely my attitude and emotional response at that particular time, I switched off the alarm and readily turned over to my sleepy state; however, I did get out of bed for the four "break of day" classes.

Immediately succeeding the last class of the morning, Cultural Anthropology, I began my journey from one state of my life, child-like stage, into a more exciting, renewing and thoroughly challenging stage, adult-like stage.

The spirit filled and enthusiastic child who thought he knew all, that I previously knew prior to attending Divine Word College Seminary, is now undergoing a new formation.

Being ignorant of and not in touch with God's moving hand, I became very confused and frustrated as to

- Who is God?
- Where I am I going in life?
- Who I am as a sexual being?
- What do friendships mean to me?
- What does the Christian faith mean to me as an individual?

Despite the fact that all these questions, among many others, seemingly clouded and darkened my outlook on life, I am now very appreciative and very grateful for the trial some and challenging experiences, that ultimately gave a new insight and strength.

For it is only through the pains and hurts of this life that I will be able to thoroughly build and possess the Christian spirit and love Christ. our Lord, and concurrently follow in the footsteps and purposeful journey of God.

Through a climactic experience in my spiritual life, that evidently instilled a new and mature spirit, faith and ultimately life, came about through a not so obvious means expressed through other significant areas of my life.

The Eucharist, in which one shares in the ultimate gift of Jesus Christ; that is, in the passion, death and resurrection, is a not so obvious means where I became fully aware, in a totally foreign and unique way, that God is love!

Relationships, increased skill in openness and freeness, a deeper and more unique faith, a greater and more consistent prayer life, and a renewed positive attitude are just five aspects of my life that were differently influenced and experienced in this transitional experience with God.

The realization came as I began to question that ideal state, "God is love" mentioned by Father Joseph Simon in the homily. If this is true, how does God express his love, and how does one know it is true?

Through the confusion and frustration, I slowly was able to penetrate the shell of death, those questions that seemingly clouded and darkened my vision.

I finally recognized that God expresses Himself through many means, such as, personal and communal prayer, the Eucharist, and most importantly, relationships with one another.

In many events of life, God challenges us to grow, but it was only until today that I realized, in a satisfying way, His challenge and power for a life expressed actively through prayer and friendships.

For example, last week a friend challenged me with a difficult problem. Unwilling to confront and accept, I began to think it was his problem, and he posed the situation out of malice.

Little did I know, it was through the friendly and loving interest and confrontation of my friend that God actually wanted to challenge, and at the same time, supply enough power so as to realize and work with that particular problem.

Today, Friday, March 9, 1984, I had a powerful experience with God, experiencing Him as a loving Father who has an influence on my life, and who has given me a new and clearer direction.

I now possess a new life, a deeper insight, and an openness that helps me to be more aware of God's love and ever-present power. It is expressed through prayer and friendships, which help confront the many beneficial barriers and obstacles along the way of life.

Succinctly, I have decisively come to accept the realization of God's love as a part of who I am, and not of who God is according to what others maintain. Previous to this experience, it was a comfortable and secure idea impressed upon me by my parents and schoolteachers as being the positive and final truth.

After I was introduced to a new college environment where the questioning of one's authority became the norm as opposed to the adherence to one's authority, there arose many questions. Through this experience I have modified and moved on from the child-like stage into a more mature and practical adult-like stage.

I no longer wear the glasses of my parents and teachers, but I now wear the glasses that are both a combination of past and present experiences, as well as authoritative experiences.

In light of this, I can, for the first time, in an actively recognizable way, distinguish the effects of God's love in two important areas of my life: prayer and, more significantly, relationships with other people.

A year later, at the end of my sophomore year in 1985, I decided to apply for the junior year abroad program. Was it another effort to flee? Perhaps on some level. But it would allow me the valuable opportunity to study in Japan for a year.

But shortly after I applied and was accepted, Grandma Clemens was diagnosed with cancer. And as Grandma Clemens had provided me with a safe haven during all those years when my abusive father had gone off the handle, she had the status of being my safe harbor in the storms that rocked much of my early life. I couldn't bear the thought of leaving her when she was sick.

I decided that I wouldn't go to Japan, but my grandmother encouraged me to go. Father Berkemeier, the parish priest who had been my inspiration, encouraged me to go as well. He reminded that the words in the Lord's prayer were, "Thy Kingdom come" and not "*My* Kingdom come." How could I argue that? And so, I went.

Japan was an astounding experience. Language acquisition was, by far, the most challenging in terms of speaking, reading, and writing. But I was there to learn the culture, and part of the culture was the language.

The other part was their religious beliefs and expressions. I found that in going there, I was this young, energetic, and optimistic guy who wanted to be a missionary and to spread the word of Catholicism and save them from themselves. Yet, the population of Japan was only 2 percent Christian. And of them, only .4 percent of them were Catholic. Once I got there, it occurred to me, "Who am I to come here and tell others what to believe?" I would quickly develop a tremendous amount of respect for the Japanese culture and their religions. There was so much honor given to one another.

I was particularly impressed by Buddhism. I saw such similarities between the Catholic Church and the Buddhist temples. We even lived in a Buddhist monastery for some time, and I slept on the floor with a tatami.

I continued to run while I was in Japan. It was a prayerful time to be open and to clear my mind. It also enabled me to experience the people and the countryside in a different manner. I was especially taken by how very communal the culture was there.

I managed to make some financial gains while I was there—though this was wholly unintentional. But one day, when I was on campus, a man came up and introduced himself to me. He was like the Ted Koppel of Japanese TV in the United States, and he wanted to keep up his English. So, he hired me for ten dollars an hour just to have conversations with him and his family. I did it, of course. This was quite a lot of money at that time. And like this TV personality, a younger woman on campus reached out for conversational English through a religious sister, and we developed an interesting relationship.

I was scheduled to stay in Japan for a year, but my grandmother was getting worse and worse. So, after six months, I returned to the United States. After coming back, my grandmother's health improved, and I was able to return to Iowa in 1986.

But it soon became clear to me and to everyone else that something in me had changed. Who can say whether it was my trip to Japan or the memories about my childhood that were drudged up when my grandmother got sick? It may not have been either of these things, or perhaps it was both. Whatever the case, the winds were definitely shifting.

chapter seven

Blowing Open the Doors

■

Back in Iowa, I befriended one of the Vietnamese students at the seminary. He was quiet and awkward, and I found him intriguing. He had been in the seminary in Vietnam and was fortunate enough to escape. But it must have been a harrowing experience. I knew I couldn't change what he had gone through, but I wanted to take care of him, nevertheless.

I found I was attracted to him on multiple levels. I was still trying to come to grips with my sexuality, and he sparked something deep inside me. For the sake of his privacy, I will call him Pin, which means "faithful boy" in Vietnamese. It is not his name, but it will suffice.

Pin aroused me in a way that other people hadn't. I wanted to be close to him, to touch him, and to take care of him. I wanted him to like me, to touch me, and to take care of me as well. Yet, those feelings both excited and frightened me at the same time. And, for whatever reason, I felt safe in being honest and open with my feelings, and he was receptive.

One weekend in 1986, Pin and I were invited to spend the weekend in Boston by an older male friend of Pin's who was interested in joining the seminary. He visited the seminary for a come-and-see weekend, and that's where we met. He wasn't my friend, and I actually didn't like him very much. Something about him made me uncomfortable, but I agreed to go with Pin anyway.

As he only had a one-bedroom apartment, he insisted that either Pin or I shared the bed with him, while the other slept on the couch. I wanted the couch, but Pin would not hear of it. In actuality, I wanted to share the bed with Pin, not this older man. Despite my reservations, I agreed to sleep in his bed. I was uncomfortable to say the least.

Shortly after the lights were out, his hands were on my stomach, and I lay still, pretending to sleep. His hands eventually traveled lower until it was clear what he had in mind. We ended up having sex. I didn't want it to happen, but I didn't know how to stop it. Though I was outgoing, I was also rather timid when it came to confrontation. It was my first time having sex, and it was anything but special or memorable. In fact, it was painful and made me feel dirty and used.

When it was over, I was upset, scared, and felt violated. I wanted to hide in the closet again, but I also wanted to flee. So, I left the man's room, grabbed Pin in the middle of the night, much like my mother had when I was young to flee the abuse of my father, and we fled to the safety of the seminary.

But something in me began to shift. It was as if the floodgates had opened. Soon after that first sexual experience, I traveled to Mississippi with a priest and psychologist from the seminary. I felt safe in talking with him about my experience. And to my surprise, he was affirming. He encouraged me to explore my sexual orientation and meet with another priest weekly for spiritual direction. He was also open and accepting to the point that I felt OK coming out of the closet.

In some way, their acceptance gave me permission to accept myself—to free myself from the deep and stifling shame about which I unaware. I suddenly felt bold, empowered, and ready to show the world who I was. The problem was, I wasn't sure what that was.

At some point in our human development, we have to develop autonomy. Most humans do this during adolescence—becoming rebellious teenagers who question everything. I say this with no shame, but I was a bit late to the game. The abuse I sustained during those early childhood years had taught me to lay low and do as I was told.

But now, there in my senior year in college, I was no longer willing to go that route. I had begun to embrace being gay, and in doing so, I started to connect with other men in the seminary. We developed our own clique where we could be out and express ourselves away from the prying eyes and ears of the others.

I quickly developed a relationship with a student from Mexico who was a little older than I was, and he was already a professed religious. He pursued me, and I was smitten with him. He was passionate yet controlling. His quick temper, combined with my personal insecurities, was a bad combination. I will spare you all the details, but it will suffice to say that while our relationship was exciting at first, it was certainly not wholesome, and it led me down a path that I would later regret.

I was beginning a dangerous chapter in my life that ushered in chaos, instability, and poor choices. I started experiencing clubbing and gay bars. There was a bar in Chicago called Little Jimmy's on Halsted where I went with a seminary friend, who was helping me transition to being OK with being gay. That first trip to a gay bar was an eye-opener.

It was dark, and there were men everywhere, freely touching one another! And it was so wonderful to be free and allowed to be completely out. I dyed my hair, changed the way I dressed, and had a strut in my step. Yes, I was feeling good about myself. The problem was, my grades were suffering and my academic performance was falling off. Plus, the many hours passed with my new friends and the late nights clubbing meant I wasn't showing up to classes.

My goal of becoming a priest took a backseat to this newfound sense of freedom and certainly jeopardized my relationship and reputation with the very religious community that had nurtured me and had provided me with security, stability, and sanity. I was lost and confused. In many ways, I wanted to embrace the life of a good seminarian, but I suppose you could say that the floodgates had opened, and I didn't know how to close them.

The timing wasn't great, to be sure. There was much more at stake in trying to find autonomy at the age of twenty-one than there would have been at the age of fifteen. But it seems it was my destiny to stage a full-blown rebellion at that time in my life.

My shift in behavior and academic performance did not go unnoticed. Especially since this was during the time when I was preparing to go to novitiate. Or at least, I was supposed to be preparing.

chapter eight

Becoming Uncloseted . . . Again

■

Father Terrence McGurk, SVD, was my German teacher in high school. We became fast friends. I revered the man. He was holy, prayerful, and constant, and he was also among those who noticed the change in me. He'd always been a loving man who cared for me and my family. Whenever we had traveled together, we would get up in the morning and pray together and celebrate mass together. But he couldn't make sense of what was changing in me.

In the meantime, I decided I could no longer be closeted. So, I came out. In my blissful ignorance, I assumed it would feel as empowering as freeing myself from that closet of my childhood. I finally said the words "I am gay" for the first time. And it was to my mom. She immediately wanted me to leave the seminary because she blamed it on the school. I refused and didn't talk to her for a few months after that. Unbeknown to me, Father McGurk had been discussing the change in my behavior and his concerns for my academic future with my mother. This upset me too.

I thought it would be freeing to come out to my mom, and it was, to some extent. But coming out is one thing. Coming out as a young man in Catholic seminary is another. In many ways,

I wish I could turn back the hands of time and spare myself, my mother, and Father McGurk from the pain I inflicted upon them with my behavior and flippant attitude. But I can't! Time marches on whether we want it to or not!

chapter nine

Duality

∎

At the age of ten, the Roman Catholic Church had opened me to the possibility of love, light, and hope, and I found it. The church had freed me, and I gave myself over to it more than willingly—making the ultimate commitment to become a priest. At the age of twenty-one, I still felt that passion and desire. But now I saw that what I thought had been unconditional love and acceptance did indeed have a stipulation. This doctrine that I fully embraced would not do the same for me. In the eyes of the church, I was a sinner. How was I to reconcile this new acceptance of myself with a doctrine that dictated I would go to hell for it? Something had to give.

Senior year in seminary is a time to prepare for going into the novitiate. Among the activities we did to prepare for this time was take a week-long retreat at the monastery. This was intended to be a time of silence, prayer, and servitude. But with my rebellion in full swing, I wasn't having any of it.

I was unwilling to miss out on any of the action my new world offered. So, I arranged to sneak out of the monastery in the middle of the night and resume the good times at the single gay bar at that time in Dubuque, Iowa. But it was becoming far too challenging to try occupying my new world and my old world at the same time. This became all too obvious on the same night when I attempted to sneak back into the monastery—with no success.

You can bet that this incident did not bode well for me going into the novitiate. In fact, it was recommended that I take a year off to get my affairs in order. I was discouraged from applying for the novitiate. As the dean of students said of me: "Chuck has come to the awareness that at this time he is not ready to apply for Novitiate. He is still dealing with the crisis of intimacy and what it means to live as a celibate. I have a concern about his lifestyle. Chuck has expensive tastes and still needs to live out a simple lifestyle. With time, I believe he will be able to live as a religious."

For a while, I agreed. Yet, there was still that lion within that was unwilling to let anyone tell me what I could and couldn't do. So, as was par for the course at this time in my life, I went right ahead and applied for the novitiate anyhow. And, of course, I was rejected.

Aimless and unmoored, I was encouraged to treat the coming year as one of discernment, prayer, and hard work, which, as you can probably guess, I had no intention of doing.

chapter ten

The Year of Living Dangerously

■

Thoroughly at odds with so much of my life, I had no intention of treating the year in earnest. I figured I'd cover the hard-work part by getting a job. From 1987 to 1988, I worked to help closedown the very high school I'd attended—Divine Word High School Seminary in Perrysburg, Ohio. It was difficult to see the place that had once provided so much comfort and support during such a formative time in my life now empty and being discarded. I did ground maintenance, a lot of packing things up, and moving them around.

I'd be stretching the truth considerably to say it was a year of hard work, especially given that many of my nights were a stream of parties. I'd take the house car, go into town, and go to the gay bar or go to dinner. My year of discernment had become my year of play. By the end of it, I'd racked up fifteen thousand dollars of credit card debt and was more lost than ever.

It was Grandma Clemens who would bring clarity back into my life.

chapter eleven

"To Where Are You Going?"

■

As 1988 progressed, I continued to tear through my life like a wannabe rockstar. Father McGurk continued to check in with my mother to share his concerns. I was still, however, unaware that he was doing this.

In the meantime, Grandma Clemens's health had taken a turn for the worst. The cancer was gaining ground, and it looked as though she was going to lose the battle. I knew I needed to spend more time with her. Just before she died on August 3, 1988, she looked at me and asked, "Chuckie, to where are you going?" I had no answer. I had once had such a clear trajectory, but now I was confused.

My grandmother died at the end of that year, and Father McGurk buried her. I met with him shortly after the funeral, apologizing for my behaviors during my senior year in college where I told him to stay the hell out of my life. That year, I was angry with him for conversing with my mother. I felt betrayed. I know he truly cared for me, but I was blinded by my own confusion and search for identity. To this day, I regret uttering those words to Father McGurk, yet strangely enough, my grandmother's death unwittingly yielded positivity where two faith-filled men agreed to never remember again.

Such clarity reentered my life; I was increasingly haunted by my last interaction with Father McGurk. I understood that it was anger that had motivated me to admonish him. I also knew better than to work from that place. I went to apologize to him, and he, ever loving and gracious, accepted my apology.

Regardless of my rage, I knew that I had to get back on track, though. I had to figure out "to where I was going," so, I moved in with my grandpa Clemens, who was now alone. He was a stable force for me at that time. He was clean-living and didn't cuss. He'd become a Catholic and was quite prayerful. He played golf and just had a peaceful demeanor that helped ground me.

My primary objective was to pay off the fifteen-thousand-dollar debt I had accrued, and I did this by working two full-time jobs, both at grocery stores. I worked hard and had little time to do anything else. I certainly had a lot of time to think, though. And during that time, I learned the value of hard work, focus, value, commitment, and being responsible. Plus, my being there helped my grandpa process the loss of the love of his life. I also learned the very valuable skill of listening.

Father McGurk died soon after that on September 9, 1989. It was a tremendous loss to my family and me, but it also felt like much of my rebellion and anger went away with his passing. I was ready to embrace whatever God had planned for me next.

chapter twelve

Not Exactly a Return to Innocence

■

I was still entertaining the idea of going back to the seminary. My call to priesthood remained strong, so I stayed active in the church and nurtured my faith. I was very busy in this role—from visiting the homebound to hospital ministry work, to liturgy, to landscaping/groundskeeping.

At this time, I met a person through mutual friends, and we seemed to get along well. Though there was a significant age difference between us, I was instantly drawn in and once again moved away from family and friends. This man was polished and relatively good-looking. He took an interest in me and, in many ways, made me feel important. He said the right things, flattered me, and appeared to encourage my vocation.

Soon, he became an important part of my life. A part of me knew I was making a mistake by becoming close to him, but another part found it exciting. The progress I had made in finding direction was slowly slipping away. Rather than learning to stand on my own feet, I was once again letting someone else take care of me. I think at some level, I saw in him the father I had always wanted.

Initially, this man treated me well. He showered me with gifts and introduced me to his family and friends. His attention made me feel good and reignited my desire to feel needed and cared for.

It didn't take long for our relationship to become sexual. Unlike my biological father, he provided me with affection, gifts, and guidance, and I ate it up. But I came to learn that his gifts had strings attached. The price of the fancy dinners and attention was about to come due.

Rather than mentoring me, he started coming into my bedroom to wake me up in the morning or to say good night. He slowly tested my receptivity to his overtures. He would linger there, making small talk. Slowly his touch became sexual, and again I was conflicted. I had worked so hard to get my life back on track, and now, this man, who was supposed to be mentoring me, was reopening a door I had worked so hard to close. Despite the promise to myself that I would turn over a new leaf, there I was again.

The whole situation was hypocritical. I gave in to sexual pleasure and passion. By no means were we boyfriends or committed to one another. He already had a partner to whom he was committed. I was just there to satisfy his needs. It was a one-way street, and only he could initiate our sexual activity. I was reminded daily of the power imbalance in our relationship. Don't get me wrong; I welcomed his advances on some level. They made me feel special and wanted, but there was no love shared between us. It was a confusing, "hot mess" that left me feeling empty, guilty, and lonely.

At the time, I tried to convince myself that I enjoyed what was happening, but I knew what we were doing was wrong. I knew he was only using me and that I would soon be discarded when he was ready to move on. On some level, I guess I also used him, or perhaps I allowed myself to be used so that I could further my goal of returning to the seminary. In the end, we both fed each other's woundedness.

I didn't realize most of these feelings at the time, of course, but after I met Harry, I saw this and many of my previous relationships in a different light. As Brian Vincent Michael Sullivan, a dear friend of mine who later became a true mentor with his lifelong partner, Bob Curtis, used to say, "Time wounds all heels."

During all of this chaos, another priest, who was involved with priestly vocations, took me on an all-expenses paid excursion to Oahu, Hawaii, for two weeks. I was still living in that rectory, and this priest wanted to get to know me better before he was willing to assign me to a seminary. Fortunately, he didn't have any sexual motives, and, in fact, he stayed at a monastery while I stayed at a hotel with another seminarian with whom I had never met. We shared little in common and ended up ignoring one another for the most part.

I was drifting back to the old behaviors that were happening before I'd pulled myself back together—partying and going to gay bars. I was lulled into a false sense of security. I thought I didn't need to hide the being-gay thing this time. I was still committed to becoming a priest, so, I told this priest that I was gay.

I was surprised when he expressed concern. And he expressed this concern with my parents too. So, I put a lid on all of the gay activities and decided once and for all that I wouldn't talk about it when I returned to the seminary. I committed myself to focusing on my studies and trying to learn how to be a good and holy priest.

I was accepted as a priestly vocation, and in August 1990, I went on to graduate seminary. I promised myself that this time, things would be different. I would learn from my mistakes and do things differently. And things were different, very different this time.

During the initial orientation, a young man named Harry caught my eye. He was a head-turner. He was quiet and not terribly engaging. And he wore a gray suit that was tailored to his firm body. His bright red hair, rosy cheeks, and beautiful smile drew me in. I assumed he wasn't a seminarian because he was so shy, but when everyone else cleared out, he was still there. He was religious, smart, and prayerful.

I went up to him and introduced myself. I was taken. He, not so much so. In fact, as we got to know each better, he was turned off by my wanting to express myself. I always wanted to show my colors, so he started calling me *Peacock*. At the time, it was not entirely a compliment—though it would eventually become one.

Although he didn't exactly like me at first, he didn't dislike me either. I think my gregarious and outgoing personality conflicted with his shy and quiet demeanor. We were opposites in so many ways, but I was drawn to him and found him intriguing. He was gay, but he didn't party, go to bars, or carry on. I wanted a physical relationship, but he clearly did not.

Despite being shy, he was warm and kind. The more he pushed me away, the more I wanted to be with him. We were both wounded souls, but we responded to our wounds in very different ways. But, thanks to my perseverance, our friendship grew, and we became close friends. It actually felt good to have someone in my life who was a positive influence for a change. We spent a lot of time together, and I like to think it was good for both of us.

It had been a while since I felt this closeness with another person without it becoming sexual. I had friends, for sure. I was outgoing and developed friendships easily, but with Harry, there was an emotional connection that was hard to explain.

So, I kept pursuing him. And one night—actually, it was my birthday, January 16, 1991—I went to his room to say goodnight and leaned in to kiss him. He turned his head away with a stunned look on his face. He didn't seem angry or upset, but he looked confused, perhaps conflicted. While I was still of the mindset that we could be sexually active and be priests, he felt the exact opposite.

During this time, Harry began to question his vocation to the priesthood. He, too, was falling in love, and it was confusing for both of us. For him, it was a new feeling. For me, it triggered fear that my history would once again repeat itself. It was something that neither of us wanted to happen, but, at the same time, neither of us was willing—or perhaps able—to stop it. The connection was set.

So, from January to May of 1991, we had regular opportunities to see one another—at outings, dinner, and prayer. Our friendship grew and flourished. He was terribly predictable with all of these, so I would always find ways to be around him. I knew where he would sit, when he would stay longer after prayer, and things like that. I made sure to include him in activities with other friends as I inserted myself into his routine.

Then, around February or March, he invited me to meet his parents. But when I got there, his parents were gone for the weekend. It was the first time we had the opportunity to be completely alone overnight, away from the seminary, away from distractions. It was just the two of us.

I think we were both a little nervous, so we went out to dinner, drank a glass of wine, and returned home to watch a movie. While we were watching the movie, I asked if I could touch his hair, and I was surprised when he said yes. That moment of intimacy lead to more. We would eventually consummate the relationship later that night in his childhood bed.

I was his first real sexual encounter, and unlike my first, it was special, almost magical for both of us. I was no virgin, as you know, but that encounter was also a first for me; I experienced the difference between lust and love. What we shared that night was far more than sex; we expressed our love for one another in a way that I had never thought possible.

At first, I was worried about how he would respond and how it would impact our relationship. He was quiet in the morning, which worried me. I could tell the wheels of his mind were turning. For me, it was wonderful. Somehow, my time with him felt special, perhaps more tender than to what I was accustomed. There was no shame or regret. And, to my surprise, Harry felt the same. Our friendship had moved to another level.

A door I promised myself that I would keep closed had once again cracked open. Although part of me wanted to slam it shut for fear of being hurt, I knew that was not possible. I was confused, so I went back to business and immersed myself in my studies, trying to push my feelings for Harry to the background. I tried to emotionally distance myself from him, but it wasn't easy.

This time, however, it was Harry who pursued me. Something in him was awakened, and he wanted to talk about it, explore it. How could I deny him?

What made Harry different from the previous men I had been involved with was his innocence and underlying wholesomeness that drew me in. He cared for me as a person. It wasn't lust or fun he was after; it was love. For once, I found someone who loved the real me. I didn't have to hide anything; I didn't have to put on a show or try to impress him. I told him my whole story, the gory details and all, and he still loved *me*. For the first time in many years, I felt safe. I felt loved.

But could I give up my calling to the priesthood?

chapter thirteen

The Fall from Grace

∎

I had known priests who had committed relationships with one another. Perhaps Harry and I could do the same. I was ready to give it a go, but Harry was another story.

He had a different view of the priesthood. I remember him saying that if he were to commit adultery, it was not going to be against God. In no way was he willing to be sexually involved with a priest or as a priest. In fact, it was during this discussion that Harry gave me an ultimatum that would forever change my life.

He had fallen in love, and for him, that precluded the priesthood. Harry informed me that he would be leaving the seminary, and he invited me to leave with him. If I stayed, our relationship would be over.

For me, the decision was not so easy. I could follow my heart and leave the security of the seminary, or I could stay, knowing that I would not be able to be with the person I loved. As I stood at the crossroads, my class was scheduled to spend six weeks in Assisi, Italy. Harry and I were in different classes, so he would remain at the seminary without me.

Leaving Harry behind, I immersed myself in prayer. He didn't rush me; he was willing to wait for me to decide. Was I truly in love, or was I mistaken? Was Harry really different from my past relationships and encounters, or was I fooling myself?

In my mind, I planned to continue my studies and part ways with Harry. Sure, it would be difficult, but I felt called to the priesthood. I'd faced pain before, and I knew that the pain would lessen over time. But, in my heart, I knew it just felt right to be with him.

I prayed for guidance, and over time, my fear was replaced with certainty; I knew my life was about to change. I remember calling Harry from Italy to share the good news. In those days, international calls were expensive, so we had to keep it short.

I had finally done it. I committed myself to beginning a new journey outside the confines of the seminary, which had dominated so much of my life. I wasn't saying no to priesthood; I was saying yes to love.

In 1991, there was no such thing as gay marriage or even domestic partnership. With my return from Italy and ultimately our departure from the seminary, we busied ourselves with planning our new lives together. We settled on a private commitment ceremony, just the two of us before God.

We traveled to Mexico and exchanged vows on August 5, 1991, the eve of the Feast of the Transfiguration of Christ, praying that Christ would transfigure our lives together.

We left the seminary, but now what? Those initial days were difficult. I moved in with my sister, and Harry lived in a summer home owned by his parents. We each secured jobs, but they were in different cities, miles apart.

We maintained our relationship from afar. I visited him every weekend, and we spoke on the phone for hours at a time. It wasn't an ideal way to begin a relationship, but it worked for us.

Having spent much of my life in the seminary, it was time for me to figure out what I wanted to do for a career. I first applied for a job in a nursing home but was told that I was overqualified.

However, the woman with whom I had interviewed took pity on me and offered to refer me to her friend at the local community mental health agency who was looking for someone to work with people who experienced severe and persistent mental illness. I got that job, and it was a good fit for me, as it allowed me to be pastoral and caring, helping make a difference in the lives of people.

Despite the challenges, my life seemed to be on a positive trajectory.

chapter fourteen

Focus, Fortitude, and Forbearance

■

Harry and I settled into a routine that worked for us. But a year later, Harry was offered a job three hours away that was too good to refuse. We decided that he should take the job and that we would continue our long-distance relationship. We were convinced our love would survive the distance.

At first, it worked. We still spent weekends together, and we spoke multiple times a day. But when you are young and in love, you want to be together, and the distance began to take its toll. We started to argue and become frustrated with one another. Although we trusted each other, we were both lonely and living miles apart. Something had to give.

It was time to take another leap of faith. If our relationship was going to survive, we had to find a way to create a home together. I left the job I loved and moved in with Harry, with little more than faith that things would work out. Fortunately, they did. I was offered another job, again in the field of mental health.

Finally, I had a home where I was valued and loved. It was far from the home life I had experienced as a child. I was truly happy and felt safe. The insecurities and instability that had once haunted me were replaced with integrity, stability, and love.

the seeds of self-destruction or SUCCESS

It was during this time of calm and stability that my stepfather died of lung cancer on August 10, 1993. The man who had made such a difference in my life had died. My mother was heartbroken, and five months later, her health deteriorated. On my twenty-ninth birthday, my mother experienced extreme and unrelenting abdominal pain. She was not one to complain, and within a few days, we learned that she had advanced colon cancer.

The news knocked the air from my lungs. I felt lost and scared and wanted to seek shelter in that closet that had brought me temporary peace as a young boy.

How could I say goodbye to the woman who was my shelter from the abuse I had experienced? I had to be strong for her sake. I had to be there for her in her hour of need.

The prognosis was poor, and my mother declined treatment. She chose to pursue palliative care and entered hospice. I was devastated.

I had just started a new career, and Harry and I were enjoying our lives together. Everything seemed to be going so well until my mother's diagnosis. But we packed up our dog, Heidi Marie, and made the three-hour drive every weekend to be with my mother.

On March 17, her health had deteriorated to the point where it was clear that her time on this earth was almost over. We made the trip back to her home to begin the long and painful process of saying goodbye. I stayed with my mother, and Harry returned to our home.

He would come visit on weekends, but I missed his loving embrace. I wanted to feel safe in his arms as I let go of my mother, but that wasn't possible.

The time I spent with my mother was cathartic. She and I were able to speak about life and the painful experiences we had shared together. We laughed, cried, and brought closure to most of the loose ends.

One memory that stands out is March 17, when Harry and I arrived at her home. My mother held court as they say. She gathered us all together, my sisters, grandparents, and an aunt, and she told us each of us how we were individually important to her and how we were loved. When it was Harry's turn, she told him that she knew I was safe in his hands and that her work on earth was complete. She knew he would protect me no matter what storms life would throw at us.

She then wanted to go and pray with just me. My sisters wanted to join us, but she wanted only me there. So, I laid down next to her, we held hands, and we prayed the Lord's Prayer. I wasn't a priest at that time, so being called upon to pray with her at that time was remarkably powerful and meaningful. I will treasure that moment with my mom forever.

On the night of March 22, my mother began calling for Jack. There was no wind or inclement weather that night, but the very special Tiffany lamp that Jack had purchased on a wedding anniversary many years before suddenly lost power. None of the other power went out. And there was nothing wrong with the wiring. When she stopped calling for Jack, the lamp went back on. She died the next day, on March 23. Harry and I were both at her side.

I had learned so much from my mother. She had prepared me for life, and I was now ready to put into practice all that she had instilled in me.

My mom was a pillar of courage, softening the blows of domestic violence, navigating the uncharted waters of pain, possibility, and potential life, and ultimately, affirming wholeness where she lived anew. When life's challenges appeared unsurmountable, she faced them with focus, fortitude, and forbearance.

Focus, for me, which I saw in my mom, is clarity of purpose. She was certain about her standing in life. *Fortitude* is about stiffening your spine. My mom always pulled herself up and stood tall. Finally, my mother demonstrated *forbearance* by checking out a situation and then moving forward with patient endurance, no matter what the obstacles.

Her love and her legacy would live on. And we would continue to learn about her even after her death. There was an incident that underscored her character, and the night before we buried, her it came to light.

On the night before my mother's funeral mass, a woman I didn't know came into the funeral home. She appeared to be homeless, wore disheveled clothing, and a had a scent that indicated she had not bathed in some time. Though nobody in town seemed to know her, they knew of her. She was something of an eccentric icon in the community. As such, when she entered the space, everyone parted ways—as this was often the response to her within the community. My grandfather and I, on the other hand, spoke with her.

The town stranger, who would not disclose her name, told us that she had come to pay her respects. After my father died, my mom had been working at the hardware store to keep her health insurance. The woman told me that my mother was the only person at the hardware store who was kind to her and who made her feel important. This, of course, did not surprise me.

We invited her to join us at mass, but she declined and then disappeared. She did show up outside of the church before mass and again at the cemetery, watching from afar. There was something in her that gave me the sense that she was ever-present, and it made me feel my mother was in good hands and fully alive.

I was reminded of the Road to Emmaus in Saint Luke's Gospel (Luke 24:13–35):

> 'That very same day, two of them were on their way to a village called Emmaus, seven miles from Jerusalem, and they were talking together about all that had happened. Now as they talked

this over, Jesus himself came up and walked by their side; but something prevented them from recognizing him. He said to them, 'What matters are you discussing as you walk along?' They stopped short, their faces downcast. Then one of them, called Cleopas, answered him, 'You must be the only person staying in Jerusalem who does not know the things that have been happening there these last few days.' 'What things?' he asked. 'All about Jesus of Nazareth,' they answered, 'who proved he was a great prophet by the things he said and did in the sight of God and of the whole people; and how our chief priests and our leaders handed him over to be sentenced to death, and had him crucified. Our own hope had been that he would be the one to set Israel free. And this is not all: two whole days have gone by since it all happened; and some women from our group have astounded us: they went to the tomb in the early morning, and when they did not find the body, they came back to tell us they had seen a vision of angels who declared he was alive. Some of our friends went to the tomb and found everything exactly as the women had reported, but of him they saw nothing.'

Then he said to them, 'You foolish men! So slow to believe the full message of the prophets! Was it not ordained that the Christ should suffer and so enter into his glory?' Then, starting with Moses and going through all the prophets, he explained to them the passages throughout the scriptures that were about himself. When they drew near

the seeds of self-destruction or SUCCESS

to the village to which they were going, he made as if to go on; but they pressed him to stay with them. 'It is nearly evening' they said 'and the day is almost over.' So he went in to stay with them. Now while he was with them at table, he took the bread and said the blessing; then he broke it and handed it to them. And their eyes were opened, and they recognized him; but he had vanished from their sight. Then they said to each other, 'Did not our hearts burn within us as he talked to us on the road and explained the scriptures to us?' They set out that instant and returned to Jerusalem. There they found the Eleven assembled together with their companions, who said to them, 'Yes, it is true. The Lord has risen and has appeared to Simon.' Then they told their story of what had happened on the road and how they had recognized him at the breaking of bread.'

This town stranger symbolized to me how, in the midst of suffering and my mother's death, faith demanded that I look beyond the grave and embrace the resurrection. In sharing her respects, the stranger reminded me of a dusty road that prepares two disciples to recognize the risen Jesus in the breaking of bread.

Isn't it interesting that when Jesus appeared to two "downcast" (Luke 24:17) disciples on resurrection day, He didn't do the very thing that would have broken into their despair—identify Himself? Just as the town stranger had not revealed herself.

As in Saint Luke's Gospel, the two disciples thought all was lost! So, when asked why these were men traveling away from Jerusalem, the answer was clear. Surely it was because Jesus's death there had deeply disappointed them. They had been "hoping that He would be the one to redeem Israel" (Luke 24:21), and that had fallen to dust and defeat. What was the point of staying in Jerusalem any longer?

Eventually, Jesus wanted the Emmaus-bound disciples to see for themselves that God had not lost control of His Creation, even in the disaster they had recently experienced in Jerusalem. No, Jesus was fully alive, as was revealed in the breaking of the bread.

When facing my mother's death, the Emmaus story as represented in the town stranger challenged my faith to look beyond death's defeat and trust that she was fully alive. Finally, my mother's legacy would carry on a purely practical level as well. The money she left us after she passed gave Harry and me enough so we could put a down payment on our first house together.

As we stared over the precipice of our new life, there was a sense of renewed birth and beginning. It was all very exciting. Of course, I had no concept at that time of just how very new, different, and challenging this next beginning would be.

Part III

LIVING LIFE ANEW
(The World of Possibilities)

chapter fifteen

Rising Above Life's Challenges

∎

Here's the big question to consider: How do you rise above a chronic and potentially debilitating condition? You go beyond yourself; you write and share; you affirm life.

That's what I'm doing here.

In 1996, I was diagnosed with multiple sclerosis. And I'll tell you, being chronically ill has been no picnic. No matter who you are, when it happens to you, your life changes dramatically. The clarion call for adaptive and/or maladaptive responses ensures positivity. Think about it: in the archaic sense of the word, receiving a diagnosis of a chronic illness challenges one's stability, life's certainty, and is a potentially humiliating experience where you become acutely aware of life's limitations and the fragility of the human body. You must severely ration your time, treasures, and talents.

A personal maxim, ascribed by my Mayo Clinic Neuropsychologist, Daniel Rohe, PhD, is, "Life's stress level is equal to resources divided by demands." In many cases, you have to rely on someone else to help you with daily tasks, an experience many find to be embarrassing, shameful, and debilitating. Personal pride often takes a huge hit and rests well in the proverbial back seat of life, as it were.

Chronic illness can seem like a curse of suffering, rejection and "being no good," but as an Old Catholic priest, suffering life's challenges can also open the door to life-giving humility, repentance, and grace.

These days, I don't call my diagnosis MS. I call it "my little friend" (though it's not little, at all), and I speak to it. I ask it not to harm me and not to take things completely away. "You can live in my body," I say, "but we must work in harmony."

chapter sixteen

Embracing "What Good Looks Like"

■

In 1992, with religious aspirations and the seminary behind me—for the time being, at least—I shifted my focus to a new career. After all, Harry and I had left our former world of absolutes in exchange for *love*. And that was great. But LOVE (capital letters or otherwise) wasn't going to provide us with food, prayer, or a roof over our heads as the seminary had since 1979. So, we needed to be practical. We needed money. It was time to search for a way to be independent.

In 1994, I started my master's in the social work program at Eastern University. I was working in community mental health at the time with great zest and gusto. I realized that I had all the religious experience, but I wanted more practical hands-on experience and to increase my academic prowess.

In 1995, while engaging in an internship on the clinical track program, I realized I wanted to have public policy exposure as part of my internship, which wasn't part of the program.

So, while in the clinical track program in 1995, I reached out to Michigan Representative Laura Baird, who was working on a project that involved research around the incidence of children with mental illness and the criminal justice system. She agreed to plug me in and assist her in achieving her outcome. Meanwhile, this would satisfy my interest in being exposed to the legislature, public policy, and state law. I wanted to know this side of dealing with the mentally ill, public policy, and to fine-tune the "art of engagement," which is better known as politics. Because to be an advocate who can speak on behalf of an individual with a mental illness, I knew I had to understand how the laws are made and how the wheels turn there. Otherwise, how could I possibly *advocatus,* or speak on behalf of others?

There was a barrier, though. Representative Laura Baird was an attorney, and I needed to have a master of social work to supervise.

How do you rise above a challenge that's on the table rather than get taken down by the "boo hoo, hoo, I can't get this done" mentality? You identify what resources or opportunities are out there to make your dream come true. I just needed to figure out where I'd find someone with a MSW who'd be willing to help.

That's when I turned to the Michigan chapter of the National Association of Social Workers and reached out to Peter Weidenaar, who was a MSW and served as the chapter's executive director. I inquired as to whether he'd be interested in supervising, and he was. But he would be more than a supervisor. He would be a mentor, a guide, and leader who truly understood what "good" looked like.

I learned five very important questions from Peter Weidenaar that I carry with me to this day:

1. What do you say?
2. For what purpose?
3. With whom?
4. How much?
5. And at what time?

Those are critical pieces to hone, fine-tune, and utilize when working in public life. Because the truth is, not everyone needs to know everything about you. As Pope John XXIII, who is now a saint, used to say, "It's unnecessary to share all that you know with everyone." Or, in my Flint interpretation, "Don't put all your junk on Front Street."

I learned so much about working in the legislature from both Laura Baird and Peter Weidenaar. One example of taking those teachings and putting them into action happened when, at one point, people in mental health—meaning clinicians, social workers, and patients—were challenged with a proposal in the Michigan's state Senate to eliminate the State Supplementation Payment of the Social Security Administration's Supplemental Security Income (SSI). SSI is Title 16 funding that is for people who haven't, for whatever reason, been able to pay into the Social Security System and who are unable to attain substantial, gainful employment through no fault of their own. When I discovered that Governor John Engler was proposing to eliminate $14 of SSI (which was around $470 at that time), I decided it was time to rally the troops.

I spoke to the mother of one of my clients who relied on this supplementation and told her we needed to go, testify, and ensure positivity. She agreed. So, we found out when the hearing would take place. I helped her to craft her testimony while I also prepared my own, and we went and spoke. We testified before three different state senators, and they listened to what we said. They reinstated that $14 in the law.

At the end of the day, my work with Representative Laura Baird and attorney Peter Weidenaar enabled me to be a participant in the process of positive change on the legislative level by gaining an understanding of the process, procedure, and language involved in public policy. In other words, it helped me understand what the hell was going on there.

Maybe it all goes back to one of my values, which is to meet a person where he or she is. I didn't know the legislative process.

How was I going to meet them where they were? By going right into the bowels of the legislature.

Another value I hold is the importance of suspending personal judgment. Rather than starting with a preconceived notion, it is important to take the time to listen and learn from the person without letting my baggage and beliefs set the stage, and thereby be a good advocate or champion.

The way I see it, you must seize life fully and at every turn. I constantly ask myself, how can I help people and myself seize this proverbial stage of life? So, although a lot of people say *carpe diem* (seize the day), I'm more inclined to say *carpe proscenium,* or "seize this stage" of life! The experience with Laura Baird allowed me to do just that. And I would continue to seize with enthusiastic vigor. I would have to.

In 1995, I began to work as an intern at Pfizer. Claire William Howe (Bill) was the Pfizer director of government relations for Michigan, Kentucky, and Ohio, and would be a key player and something of a mentor throughout my life. I was so excited to begin my internship with him. He represented corporate America and an opportunity to succeed.

The first day, I was to start at 8:00 a.m. I gave myself enough time to get there but was delayed by a stalled train. When I strolled into the office, it was 8:15 a.m. "Good morning, Bill," I called as I walked to my office.

"Good morning," he called back.

A short amount of time passed. Then he came to my door.

What is important and specific to Bill is that he taught through the Socratic approach. He would ask questions to drive home a point, to teach a lesson and affirm a positive outcome.

"Charles," Bill said. "I have a question for you."

"Yeah, sure, Bill," I responded.

"Are you starting the morning shift or the afternoon shift? Because, you know, at Pfizer, we have a standard. It's Pfizer time.

And Pfizer time is such that if you are to be here at eight o'clock, then you are here at seven forty-five."

Such was the beginning of my career space at Pfizer. You can bet I never once arrived after 7:45 a.m. again. And Bill taught me how to behave, how to manage the endless opportunities that Pfizer would—unbeknown to me at the time—provide, and thrive within my newfound corporate world. I began to see a different world that opened to meeting people, and to managing my own personal needs and be accepted, recognized, and valued. That was all tempered by my life experiences with him.

Within that year, I would travel with Bill to a luncheon in Ohio and be seated at a table with people who were all high-level executives and government officials. Then there was me. We were each required to talk about "what we do." Before I knew it, I was deep in the weeds of my personal story, and I couldn't stop talking. Finally, Bill stepped in and said simply, "Charles works with me as a paid intern in my office." That finished the story for me.

Bill and I processed that afterward. I had experienced the tension that comes with being asked a question and the desire to be recognized and validated. I needed to learn a lot about balancing the personal and the professional.

You see, those five very important questions that I carry with me to this day have yet to root themselves within my body, mind, and soul. They seem to be constantly tempered by "my little friend" called MS:

1. What do you say?
2. For what purpose?
3. With whom?
4. How much?
5. And at what time?

My internship evolved a year later into a contractual lobbyist position, where Bill Howe hired me to work for Pfizer part time. I worked in that position until 1999, when I shifted to a full-time pharmaceutical sales representative. I had come to sales from the world of Bill Howe and government relations, and I was now "carrying the bag," as they say. My goal was to learn the front line of Pfizer in terms of how they generated corporate revenues to keep the multibillion-dollar company alive. The answer was the products. The first two years, I was a full-time employee, but I was required to complete four phases of training.

Where the roads of government relations and sales came to meet happened the first week of my job in sales. Bill Howe called. "How's it going out there, Charles?" he asked.

"Great!" I said, expounding on everything I loved, appreciated, and knew about blood pressure management, infectious disease, and erectile dysfunction.

"I have a question for you," he said. "If ever you're called before a grand jury and they ask you this question, how would you respond?"

"What's the question, Bill?"

"Have you ever given your samples, your starters, to a nonprescriber? How would you respond?"

"No," I said, though partially incensed by such a question.

"Good," he said. "Keep it that way." And then he hung up.

Bill Howe was mindful of the space of sales and that you should always guard your words and actions. Don't deviate. Don't become a person who will give samples to your friends and family. And certainly, do not give anyone anything that would harm your "backside of life," as it were.

For me, this was the meeting of the two worlds between policy/government relations and sales, measured against what's expected of us.

the seeds of self-destruction or SUCCESS

In my sales career, I would achieve the top 10 percent of sales in the company. This was the pinnacle of success in Pfizer. I achieved this three times in my time there. And once, I was number one in the country with one of our drugs. I won trips, money, and accolades during this glorious time. But part of what had made this all the more glorious was what had happened three years earlier.

On a cold, wintry morning in January of 1996, I awoke and went outside to retrieve the newspaper. As I did so, I fell on our slightly sloped driveway that was covered in ice from the night before. Little did anyone know or suspect, that fall signaled my life's greatest challenge was lurking on the horizon.

Stunned by the fall, lying on my back only in my underwear and a T-shirt and hoping against hope to be concealed by the morning's darkness, I cried out in pain.

"What must I do now?" I asked myself. "To where do I go?"

In the days and weeks ahead, sensory loss began to invade my body. It started in my legs and expanded out from there to my face and arms. I began to have some difficulty with walking and was beginning to experience some visual disturbance. My fingers would go numb. But it was only when the sensory loss went to my peritoneal area (yes, I am a man) that I thought, "Oh no, this can't be. I need to go to the doctor."

The first doctor to whom I went was my cousin, who was a chiropractor. He was somebody I revered and respected. He and his brother, Jeffrey, were smarter than whips while we were growing up, and we used to play with one another. They had resided on the west side of Flint, while I lived on the other side. They enjoyed reading the *Encyclopedia Britannica* from beginning to end. They knew that their mother and father loved them, cared for them, and respected them. Life had been good to them in those early years of life.

So, in my hour of need, I thought I would reach out to Tommy. He adjusted my spine and took the necessary X-rays, concluding with, "I hope this helps, Chuckie. But if there's no improvement, you'll need to see your family doctor!"

The constellation of sensory loss continued, and my worries increased as to my personal well-being—all of this on the heels of my mother having passed away. I decided to reach out to my family physician. As she was out of town, I turned to another friend who happened to be a physician at Michigan State University.

I made the appointment and saw him as scheduled. He examined my body and asked all the appropriate questions. He then concluded, "You know, Charlie. This is a bizarre constellation of symptoms. In falling, if you injured your back here," he began, pointing to the center of his back, "we would see evidence of it over here," he added, pointing to his leg. "So, I'm not sure what's going on here, and I'd like you to have additional tests."

One of those tests was an MRI. While he was attempting to order it, the nurse peered into the room and said, "The insurance is refusing and won't approve." Dr. Gerard proceeded to take the phone, giving me a "preemptive disclaimer." He nodded to me. "Charlie, I have to say this to get it approved," he assured me, then went on to say it to the insurance company. I did feel a certain amount of reassurance until he added, "I need this MRI to rule out brain cancer."

My heart fell.

Although he had reassured me that his words were all necessary for the approval process and there was no reason to worry, I wasn't quite buying it. The MRI was scheduled for the next day, and so I returned home, anxious and concerned about what it would reveal.

I'd gotten home early in the afternoon and was surprised when Harry pulled into the driveway, home from work early. He had left work to see how my appointment had gone.

"Did someone call you?" I asked him.

He looked concerned. "No. Were they supposed to?"

It was so strange, his coming home early that day. It was as if he had a sixth sense that something was wrong. I started to tell him about the events that afternoon when the phone rang. The MRI had been rescheduled for 6:30 p.m. that evening.

Harry and I went to the hospital early that evening. The MRI was supposed to be for the spine only to figure out why I was having so many issues in my legs and arms. While closed into that narrow tube, I heard a thumping sound. Concerns of brain cancer whirled around in my mind, and I wondered if this was what it was like to be dead—with this bright white light enveloping me. I began to wonder if I was going to be dead soon and if this was how it would be.

In the meantime, questions kept coming in through the audio: "Are you OK, Mr. Blanchard?" OK was the last thing I was, but I told them I was fine. I was in there for about two hours when they finally brought me out and allowed me to go to the restroom.

When I exited the tube, the doctor was there with Harry. He told me to head to the restroom to relieve myself and that we'd talk when I returned. I went to the bathroom, and when I stepped back into room, I got a sinking feeling in my stomach when I saw that Harry had red-rimmed eyes and was trying hard not to cry. He embraced me as the doctor gently said, "Charlie, I think you have brain cancer, and the prognosis will not be good. But we're just not sure what's going on. So, we want to do your brain now."

Shaken and scared, I got back into the tube. It was a painful experience because it was now clear they were going after something I didn't want to face.

How was life going to be for me? For Harry? What would the future look like?

I was certain I was meeting my end. After that ordeal was over, I was told that the doctor would call later that evening to discuss the results after he consulted with the radiologist.

Harry and I gathered our stuff and left the hospital.

It was a painful wait. We feared for the worst, but Harry put on a brave face and encouraged me to be positive. "Let's pray for a miracle," he encouraged.

Soon afterward, the call came. "I have good news," the doctor said. "It's not cancer. It's MS."

I'll admit that I felt a tremendous relief at hearing this news. "We have other tests we want to run to confirm this," he said. So, I was scheduled for a spinal puncture at McClaren Hospital in Lansing the next day.

In this arduous medical procedure (which would be among the first of many), I received a local anesthetic, and they showed me the very long needle they would use to pull fluids from my spine.

With Harry at my side, I tried being calm. They said I needed to be very still to avoid the possibility of paralysis. Oh, sure. OK. No problem. In those fluids, though, they found derivatives of the brain, which confirmed that I did, in fact, have MS.

The next day, we met with the doctor, who said "I could send you to a local neurologist, but I'm not doing that. I want you to have the best medicine and treatment possible, so, I'm arranging for you to go to the Mayo Clinic. These are the best minds in the world, and they will be familiar with a case like yours." I think it was this good fortune and God's providential care that allow me to walk, talk, and breathe today.

I think back to the relief I felt at having an MS diagnosis over brain cancer. And yes, it was certainly the more desirable diagnosis of the two, in terms of long-term prognosis. But my life was about to change in ways that only those with chronic illness can grasp. I would soon be engaged in what I now call the show-and-go dance with my little friend called MS.

Those first two years of my diagnosis, while I was thriving at Pfizer, with my MS diagnosis, it was like I was living a rockstar life. I was lulled into believing that MS wouldn't overpower me. But in the summer of 1998, the MS began to demonstrate just how unfriendly it could be.

I woke up one morning and wasn't able to find the floor. I would hobble around without feeling the floor underneath my feet. I had no sense of walking. I let this go on for probably about a week until I finally called my doctor at the Mayo Clinic. She called in 3,000 mg of Solu-Medrol IV steroids that were to be administered at a local hospital.

This is where and when I first posed the question at the beginning of this chapter: How do you rise above a chronic and potentially debilitating condition?

I continued to work at Pfizer, learning, meeting with doctors, and traveling multiple miles every day. Then, in 2004, having spent almost four years employing social work skills as a pharmaceutical sales representative, my district manager would help me in a way that I had never imagined he would. Up until that magical year, I'd been doing a lot of activity with a lot of physicians, but I wasn't "winning." Everything I did repeatedly landed me in the middle of the road. So, I asked him what I could do differently. He challenged me to embrace the 80/20 rule that, in the world of business, was as good as gospel. The 80/20 rule says that 80 percent of your business comes from the top 20 percent of potential. Now, with my background in social work and the seminary, I'd always regarded the 80/20 rule as, with all due respect, bullshit. I always assumed that if I just talked about a good product enough with enough people, I'd eventually win. But no!

The idea is, rather, to talk only to people who can deliver for you. So, I committed to that. And voila! That's when I started winning! I'm not sure what's to be gleaned here, but surprises are to be expected when transitioning from the world of absolutes to the world of possibilities. I sure didn't know. I suppose it taught me the importance of relying on people who understand spaces that aren't familiar to me and knowing how to trust them.

By 2008, I'd made so many connections and contacts in New York from my Pfizer trips there that I decided I wanted to work there. My contacts in both the sales side of Pfizer and the worldwide alliance development crafted a position where I'd be working in both sales and corporate affairs. I was suddenly living the life of Riley. I moved to New York City, where I lived in Trump Towers, of all places, and had an office on Forty-Second Street between Second and Third Avenues. Pfizer footed the bill for *everything*. I received a stipend each month, and all of my expenses were paid. Harry was flown in twice per month and I was flown back to Michigan twice per month. I was expected to only do my job.

Meanwhile, I built up relationships with third-party patient advocacy groups. It was an amazing time. But after six months, it was over. My position was not going to be renewed, and I would have to return to Michigan. I was assured it was nothing I had done. Now, of course, I left the office and pored through my brain, trying to figure out where I had made a mistake. I went down the rabbit hole of being a bad boy, no good, a bag of dirt, and thinking they needed to throw me to the curb.

But who wouldn't?

As much as I had wanted to plant myself in corporate affairs, it wasn't meant to be. The reason they weren't going to renew my position was that the entire team was being eliminated due to corporate reshuffling. My return to Michigan would safeguard my career. It had nothing to do with my performance. My secondment was over.

Fortunately, or perhaps by divine intervention, a position opened near our home, so I moved back to a promoted pharmaceutical sales position in 2008 and would work in that position until October 6, 2011.

the seeds of self-destruction or SUCCESS

It was also in 2011 when I'd taken to ironically referring to my MS as my little friend. Harry had departed for Chile, where he would be for six weeks working on his master's degree and proficiency in Spanish.

I continued to work, but I was having significant issues in terms of motivation and connectedness, fatigue, and weight loss. I didn't want to look at any of it. But others were seeing it. It certainly didn't go unnoticed at work. It was clear that plans were afoot to eliminate me from my position.

When Harry came back after that six weeks, he looked me square in the eyes and asked me what was going on.

"What do you mean?"

"You look terrible, Charlie," he said with a look of deep concern. "Please. You need to get medical attention. Don't put this off."

Seeing Harry's expression was enough to convince me to head to the doctor. But little did I know that Harry called Paul and Mark as well as Jim and Fred, inquiring as to what they knew. You see, they were true friends who understood "what good looks like."

The doctor immediately placed me on medical leave, thus protecting my job. I was afraid I was about to be fired as my performance was suffering because of this disease.

Our new medical doctor ran tests, and then I was back at the Mayo Clinic. Again. New tests were showing cognitive impairment. I would need to be put on temporary disability, which turned into long-term disability.

Despite all of this, I was gunning to get back to work. My thinking was that as long as I could keep going, the disease couldn't catch me. I was clearly in denial, though. It already had.

While on short-term disability, Harry and I showed up to a government relations luncheon. My longtime friend, mentor, and trusted colleague, Bill Howe, gently took me aside, looked at me in much the same way Harry had, and the necessary change began.

"You don't look good," he said. "It's clear to me that you're unwell." And just as he'd helped me transition into Pfizer, Bill Howe would ultimately help me transition out of the company as well. "It's time to go," he finally said.

I was, at long last, able to admit that this was the case.

chapter seventeen

"Where There Are No Resources, Create Them"

■

Of course, leaving Pfizer and moving into the next chapter of my life brought many changes. I won't elaborate on this too much. I'm sure that you, as the reader, have a sense of what those changes look like.

I will say, however, that I am constantly reminded of how relationships—*all* relationships—evolve over the breadth of time. My relationship with Harry is no different. And as my little friend called MS frequents our collective doorstep, its impact grows ever more apparent—particularly in the cognitive decline. In essence, my capacity to process is increasingly challenged.

Over the years, Harry has had to take a more active role in many areas of our life together. The once shy, reserved man with whom I had fallen in love took on new and added responsibilities. Up until this time, he let me shine. I took care of our finances, yard maintenance, and arranged social events. Harry, on the other hand, spent his time cooking, cleaning, and nurturing and supporting me. He made sure I remembered what I had scheduled, that I had a warm meal, and that we had a safe place to be together as a family. We had achieved a balance that provided stability.

This disease disrupted that balance. Harry was called upon to take on more and more responsibilities, and he did. He began arranging social gatherings and started to shepherd me to make sure I didn't drop the ball. Publicly, no one knew our roles had changed, but behind the scenes, Harry assumed the role of a parent or caretaker at times, while remaining my partner in life.

In all this change, we also found peace. The foundation we had built together kept our lives from crumbling in the face of such radical change.

My resourcefulness, capabilities, and independence have waned as a result of my little friend. And as Harry has assumed this more active role, I've had to balance it with letting go. Conflicted feelings surely emerged—with inadequacy, with not being good enough, and with not being capable of placing in the top three positions. My insistence that I could still do it all led to situations like late payments, unpaid bills, the lights getting turned off, and let's just say less-than-stellar credit. Thus, Harry takes care of our finances now. And since knowing where people, events, and the things of life begin and end are challenging for me, he now schedules social events and plans vacations too.

These days, I thoroughly understand and admit there is damage to my brain. It's clear to me that the connections cannot be sped up. But I can work on my efficiencies through adaptive measures. And one of the biggest adaptive measures was admitting and accepting this. There is no sense in living in the rabbit hole. I realized I had to move forward and adjust to the change in the rhythm of my life—both personally and professionally. I needed to focus on the adaptive, versus the maladaptive. But I never forget for even one second how blessed I am to have Harry in the navigator's seat.

And in this period of transition, a door we both thought was forever closed, cracked open. Shortly before leaving active employment, Harry and I learned about the Old Catholic Church through a friend in Canada. The Old Catholic Church shares a similar theology as the Roman Catholic Church but has a much more progressive application of the faith. That door we once though forever closed was reopened. Priesthood was a possibility within the Old Catholic Church. We didn't have to hide our love. We didn't have to hide our sexuality. We could be openly gay, married, and still be welcomed into full participation of the ministry and sacraments in the faith we both love.

It was like another answered prayer. While this little friend of mine took its toll on my body, my spirit was lifted with a return to religious studies. Harry and I were ordained to the priesthood in the Old Catholic Church on December 12, 2012, and we founded Christ the Good Shepherd Old Catholic Church in Ferndale, Michigan, on May 13, 2013. Our little church, "the small church with a big heart," started with seven people and has grown to a thriving parish in Berkley, Michigan, where all are welcome and valued without exception.

My ability to be ordained to the priesthood after all the twists and turns my life has followed has been a blessing. It is clear that "Where there are barriers, you and I will indeed surmount." Never in my wildest dreams did I ever believe that I would achieve my life-long calling to the priesthood, which began at the young age of thirteen. While my love for Harry led me to leave the seminary, it was the same love that reopened the door to ministry within the Catholic faith. God is indeed good.

All of this now brings me full circle by addressing my initial question at the opening of this third part: "How do you rise above a chronic and potentially debilitating condition?"

Here is how I do it. I have devised four personal ways of managing life's challenges, and thereby avoiding life's "hot messes." The first way is what I call Embracing Charlie's new light: rules by which to live." These are self-imposed rules by which I live, and they are as follows:

Rule #1: SEE

The first rule is to keep both myself and others safe while operating with a degraded brain. SEE is an acronym for **S**top, **E**valuate, and **E**nsure. Before I speak or take any action, I need to stop, evaluate, and ensure that what I'm about to say and do is appropriate.

Rule #2: SSS

This is the not the nefarious stuff of Hitler's time. The SSS in this case stands for **S**tand, **S**top, then **S**tart walking. Because my gait is disturbed from MS, consciously standing and then stopping for a moment before I start to proceed helps with walking and avoiding gait disturbance.

Rule #3: Engaging with People

Introduction of personal content is especially hard for me. Thus, I have learned to say, "Just to let you know, if I'm slow to respond, I'm reviewing my thoughts before responding."

Rule #4: In Case of an Emergency

In case of an auto accident or emergency, call 911 first, immediately, and always. There is no deviation from this. I am not to call Harry, not the insurance company, not anyone else. Only 911.

Rule #5: "The Door Is Closed"

In meeting a person on the street, I have to remember that my personal door is closed. In other words, if I meet someone on the fly or out while walking, I need to be respectful and kind, and I need to contain myself because of the compromised executive function I experience. I have to be careful about the extent to how involved I become in other's lives. Where do I begin and where do I end? Where do you begin and where do you end? It's hard for me to connect the dots and fully understand what a person really needs and wants. I want to fix and help people, and I have to be careful to not get too involved.

Rule #6: Trust Your Instincts and Intuition

This is just another level of engagement. So, even though the door is closed in number five, there's part of me that doesn't believe it. I have to be comfortable with that sixth sense that's telling me when something isn't safe.

Rule #7: Refrain from Hugging

When multiple movements are required for hugging in a professional environment, just don't do it. Bottom line for rule seven is to guard myself mentally, physically, and professionally.

These rules are often subject to modifications during the sundowner hours when my MS acts up the most. For example, I usually add a *W* to rule number one during these hours. And the *W* stands for **W**rite.

Thus, I know if I'm going to talk and open up my big mouth during sundowner's time, I need to practice SEE with writing. So, I do all of the actions of SEE, then I write, and then I *might* speak. If I don't follow the modification where executive capabilities are required during sundowners, then I might as well just do SEE and then shut the hell up.

The second part of how I manage life's challenges is by engaging the "best minds of medicine," whether near or far.

The third part of my management plan consists of living in the moment through prayer, meditation, and reading—thereby nurturing certitude, conviction, and courage.

- It means the *certitude* to speak when it would be easier to be silent.
- It means the *conviction* to step forward when it would be easier to stay back.
- It's the *courage* to do what you don't feel or think you can and do it anyways.

Finally, I now know all too well the importance of surrounding myself with an **A**mazing **N**umber of **G**ifts, **E**mbracing **L**ove (ANGELs). Saint Paul defines love as wanting the good for another. Two defining questions include:

- Who are the people in my life who want this?
- Who are the people I love and trust and who love me back?

These are the folks who hold on to what good looks like in my life. They are the living beings of my life who are trusted. They embrace and fulfill the maxim I subscribe to that says, surround myself with people who love me, who are competent—and for whom I want only the best.

And there you have it.

chapter eighteen

Who Are Your ANGELs?

■

The primary reason I have been able to overcome the challenges I've faced in life is because of the people with whom I am surrounded, my ANGELs. The times when I floundered and made a continuing series of mistakes were the times when I pushed away from the people who cared, who had my best interests at heart, and people who were competent. Sometimes it is difficult to distinguish whether someone is an ANGEL or if he or she has ulterior motives, but when you find an ANGEL, hold on to him or her.

On a personal level, those people range from my mother and my grandparents, to priests and religious sisters, to the wonderful friends who have graced my life, and most importantly, to Harry.

Professionally, I have sought out people who are competent in the area of specialty. I've selected doctors and therapists who cared and who were competent in their fields, whether they were around the corner or across the country. I've also fired doctors who I felt were not available to me or who refused to think outside of the box, as they say. Convenience is not necessarily competence.

I have spoken a lot about Harry in this book, but he has truly been a transformational presence, my primary ANGEL in life. Is he perfect? Absolutely not. He has made mistakes like all of us, but even in those mistakes, he has loved me, and I have loved him.

I have tested that love on many occasions with my stubbornness and sometimes with poor choices. In the last number of years, my health challenges have not been easy for him, I am sure. But he has stood with me through it all.

I am sure I would not have met the success I have had in life without Harry at my side. As you've read, I was floundering in life, repeating the same mistakes before I met him. I think sometimes God puts people in our lives for a reason. It is important to recognize who those people are that really have our best interests at heart. When you find your "Harry," cling to him or her. We all need a stable and loving person in our lives.

At the same time, it is important to also be an ANGEL for that person and for others you meet in life as well.

So just as I opened this third part with a question, I'd like to close it—and the entirety of this meditation on my life—with another: Who are your trusted ANGELs?

If you carry this question with you through your life and stay forever aware of your own angels, you can't go wrong.

I promise.

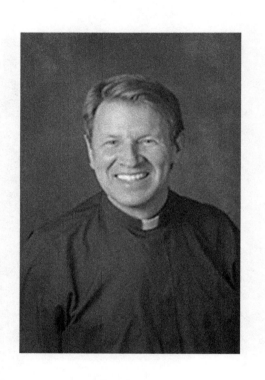

Acknowledgments

A book as big and broad as *The Seeds of Self-Destruction or Success* is indeed possible because of the focus, fortitude and forbearance of many, many people who supported me and who, in many cases, had to wait a long time to see any positivity.

I especially need to thank some of my trusted ANGELs who met me where I was in life; suspended personal judgment, and walked collectively, creating many memory moments nurturing life's faith, hope, and love:

Right Reverend Harry R. Posner Jr.
Sister Dorothy Ederer, OP
Reverend Father Lloyd S. Cunningham, SVD, PsyD
Stephanie Roupp
Gilbert David Bowlin
Mark J. Spencer
Paul S. Baker
Most Reverend Michael A. Goddard
Reverend Father Michael A. Cadotte
Catherine J. Hearsch
John P. Hearsch
Lisa E. Brent
Sherry L. Harkins
Judith R. Posner
Harry R. Posner Sr.
Helen Clemens
Donald Clemens
Victor H. Smith Jr.

Shirley Smith
Susan Posner
Robert W. Curtis
Brian Vincent Michael Sullivan
Claire W. Howe
Nina M. Hill, PhD
Janet K. Narich
Olga R. Narich
James Stokes
Frederick Hoffman
Leslie J. Hall
Reverend Father Henry W. Berkemeier
Brother Donald Champagne, SVD
Reverend Father Robert Jones, SVD
Reverend Father Wilbur Klunk, SVD
Reverend Father Terrence McGurk, SVD
Reverend Father Lawrence Mack, SVD
Reverend Father Eugene Stoll, SVD
Reverend Father James Bergin, SVD
Reverend Father Ed Tuohy, SVD, PhD
Reverend Father James Mullaley, SVD
Brother Bernie Spitzley, SVD
Reverend Father James Braband, SVD
Reverend Father Elmer Elsbernd, SVD
Brother Longinus Posch, SVD
Brother Gerard Pashia, SVD
Reverend Father Robert Johnson, SVD
Brother Thomas Granfield, SVD
Brother Gerard Raker, SVD
Brother Dominic Nigro, SVD
Reverend Father Gerald Ploof
Reverend Father David Preuss, OFM
Very Reverend J. J. Mech

Regina Simone, DO
Steven Katzman, DO
Robert Pace, MD
Claudia F. Lucchinetti, MD
Daniel Rohe, PhD
Patricia Moylan, PhD
Patricia E. Kefalas Dudek

And many others who are too numerous to mention.

Bibliography

[1] "Erik Erikson's Theory of Psychosocial Development, Stage 1," Envision Your Evolution, last modified November 17, 2019, http://www.envisionyourevolution.com/human-development/erik-erickson-theory-of-psychological-development/5453/.

[2] "Erik Erikson's Theory of Psychosocial Development, Stage 2," Envision Your Evolution, last modified November 17, 2019, http://www.envisionyourevolution.com/human-development/erik-erickson-theory-of-psychological-development/5453/.

[3] "Erik Erikson's Theory of Psychosocial Development, Stage 3," Envision Your Evolution, last modified November 17, 2019, http://www.envisionyourevolution.com/human-development/erik-erickson-theory-of-psychological-development/5453/.

[4] "Erik Erikson's Theory of Psychosocial Development, Stage 4," Envision Your Evolution, last modified November 17, 2019, http://www.envisionyourevolution.com/human-development/erik-erickson-theory-of-psychological-development/5453/.

About the Author

Father Charles Blanchard is an Old Catholic priest, a wisdom guide, and along with Father Harry Posner, Jr. is a founder of Christ the Good Shepherd Old Catholic Church.

WHERE THERE ARE BARRIERS, YOU AND I WILL INDEED SURMOUNT! has been Father Charles' modus operandi throughout his years in seminary (1979-1991), career within psychiatry (1991-99) and most recently within the pharmaceutical industry (1996-2011) which prematurely ended due to his "Little Friend" called Multiple Sclerosis.

Born in Flint, Michigan, Father Charles, who felt called to the priesthood ever since Saint Mary's Elementary School, engaged in the following educational pursuits:

- Divine Word College (1983-1987) earning a Bachelor of Arts in Philosophy and a Minor in Cross-Cultural Studies.
- Nanzan University (1985-86) completing a Junior Year Abroad Program in Japanese Culture and Language Certificate.
- St Mary's Hospital (1989-90), earning a Clinical Pastoral Education Certificate.

- Sacred Heart Major Seminary (1990-1991) pursuing a Master's in Divinity Degree.
- Eastern Michigan University (1994-1998) earning a Master's in Social Work with concentration in Mental Illness and Chemical Dependency.

Today, despite life's challenges, Father Charles finds priestly ministry rewarding whereby he engages the marginalized, disenfranchised, and oppressed. He is multi-lingual speaking Japanese, German, Latin, Spanish and English; appreciates cultural diversity; and espouses a firm belief in the empowerment model, meeting people where they are in life, suspending personal judgment and seeing the world from her/his vantage point.

Through prayer, discernment, and God's unfailing Grace, Father Charles and his husband journeyed forward, completed their seminary studies, founded Christ the Good Shepherd Old Catholic Church on May 12, 2013, and began the invitation of Peace and Love to all God's people.

May "the seeds of self-destruction or SUCCESS" serve as common ground through which we collectively walk together to challenge, inspire, and nurture the mind, body, and spirit.

CPSIA information can be obtained
at www.ICGtesting.com
Printed in the USA
LVHW030403090223
739019LV00006B/303